MW00587694

HELP,
THANKS,
WOW

ALSO BY ANNE LAMOTT

NONFICTION

Operating Instructions:
A Journal of My Son's First Year

Bird by Bird:
Some Instructions on Writing and Life

Traveling Mercies:
Some Thoughts on Faith

Plan B: Further Thoughts on Faith

Grace (Eventually):
Thoughts on Faith

Some Assembly Required:
A Journal of My Son's First Son
(with Sam Lamott)

FICTION
Hard Laughter
Rosie
Joe Jones
All New People
Crooked Little Heart
Blue Shoe
Imperfect Birds

HELP,

THANKS,

WOW

The Three Essential Prayers

ANNE LAMOTT

RIVERHEAD BOOKS
a member of Penguin Group (USA) Inc.
New York
2012

Published by the Penguin Group
Penguin Group (USA) LLC
375 Hudson Street
New York, New York 10014

USA · Canada · UK · Ireland · Australia
New Zealand · India · South Africa · China

penguin.com
A Penguin Random House Company

The author gratefully acknowledges permission to quote from:
Translation of verses by Rumi © Coleman Barks.
"Late Fragment" from *All of Us* by Raymond Carver © 1988;
1989 © Tess Gallagher.

ISBN 978-1-159463-129-0

Printed in the United States of America
10

BOOK DESIGN BY AMANDA DEWEY

For Sarah Chalfant
and
Jake Morrissey

Does sunset sometimes look like the sun is
    coming up?
Do you know what a faithful love is like?

You're crying; you say you've burned yourself.
But can you think of anyone who's not
hazy with smoke?

—Rumi

PRELUDE

Prayer 101

I do not know much about God and prayer, but I have come to believe, over the past twenty-five years, that there's something to be said about keeping prayer simple.

Help. Thanks. Wow.

You may in fact be wondering what I even mean when I use the word "prayer." It's certainly not what TV Christians mean. It's not for display purposes, like plastic sushi or neon. Prayer is private, even when we pray with others. It is communication from the heart to that which surpasses understanding. Let's say it is communication from one's heart to God. Or if that is too triggering or ludicrous a concept for you, to the Good, the force that is beyond our comprehension but that in our pain or supplication or relief we don't need to define or have proof of or any established contact with. Let's say it is what the Greeks called the Really Real, what lies within us, beyond the scrim of our values, positions, convictions, and wounds. Or let's say it is a cry from deep within to Life or Love, with capital L's.

Nothing could matter less than what we call this force. I know some ironic believers who call God Howard, as in "Our Father, who art in Heaven, Howard be thy name." I called God Phil for a long time, after a Mexican bracelet maker promised to write "Phil 4:4–7" on my bracelet, Philippians 4:4–7 being my favorite passage of Scripture, but got only as far as "Phil" before having to dismantle his booth. Phil is a great name for God.

My friend Robyn calls God "the Grand-mothers." The Deteriorata, a parody of the Desi-derata, counsels us, "Therefore, make peace with your god, / Whatever you conceive him to be— / Hairy thunderer, or cosmic muffin."

Let's not get bogged down on whom or what we pray to. Let's just say prayer is communication from our hearts to the great mystery, or Goodness, or Howard; to the animating energy of love we are sometimes bold enough to believe in; to something unimaginably big, and not us. We could call this force Not Me, and Not Preachers Onstage with a Choir of 800. Or for convenience we could just say "God."

Some of you were taught to pray at bedtime with your parents, and when I spent the night at your houses, I heard all of you saying these terrifying words: "Now I lay me down to sleep, I pray the Lord my soul to keep. If I should die before I wake . . ."

Wait, *what?* What did you say? I could die in my *sleep?* I'm only seven years old. . . .

"I pray the Lord my soul to take."

That so, *so* did not work for me, especially in the dark in a strange home. Don't be taking my soul. You leave my soul right here, in my fifty-pound body. Help.

Sometimes the first time we pray, we cry out in the deepest desperation, "God help me." This is a great prayer, as we are then at our absolutely most degraded and isolated, which means we are nice and juicy with the consequences of our best thinking and are thus possibly teachable.

Or I might be in one of my dangerously good moods and say casually: "Hey, hi, Person. Me again. The princess. Thank you for my sobriety, my grandson, my flowering pear tree."

Or you might shout at the top of your lungs or whisper into your sleeve, "I hate you, God." That is a prayer, too, because it is real, it is truth, and maybe it is the first sincere thought you've had in months.

Some of us have cavernous vibrations inside us when we communicate with God. Others are more rational and less messy in our spiritual sense of reality, in our petitions and gratitude and expressions of pain or anger or desolation or praise. Prayer means that, in some unique way, we believe we're invited into a relationship with someone who hears us when we speak in silence.

We can pray for things ("Lord, won't you buy me a Mercedes-Benz"). We can pray for people ("Please heal Martin's cancer." "Please help me not be such an asshole"). We may pray for things that would destroy us; as Teresa of Ávila said,

"More tears are shed over answered prayers than unanswered ones." We can pray for a shot at having a life in which we are present and awake and paying attention and being kind to ourselves. We can pray, "Hello? Is there anyone there?" We can pray, "Am I too far gone, or can you help me get out of my isolated self-obsession?" We can say anything to God. It's all prayer.

Prayer can be motion and stillness and energy—all at the same time. It begins with stopping in our tracks, or with our backs against the wall, or when we are going under the waves, or when we are just so sick and tired of being psychically sick and tired that we surrender, or at least we finally stop running away and at long last walk or lurch or crawl toward something. Or maybe, miraculously, we just release our grip slightly.

Prayer is talking to something or anything with which we seek union, even if we are bitter or insane or broken. (In fact, these are probably the best possible conditions under which to pray.) Prayer is taking a chance that against all odds and past history, we are loved and chosen, and do not have to get it together before we show up. The opposite may be true: We may not be able to get it together until after we show up in such miserable shape.

But in any case, we are making contact with something unseen, way bigger than we could ever imagine in our wildest dreams, even if we are the most brilliant, open-minded scientists and physicists of our generation. It is something we might dare to call divine intelligence or love energy (if there were no chance that anyone would ever find out about this). Prayer is us— humans merely being, as e. e. cummings put it— reaching out to something having to do with the eternal, with vitality, intelligence, kindness, even when we are at our most utterly doomed and skeptical. God can handle honesty, and prayer begins an honest conversation.

My belief is that when you're telling the truth, you're close to God. If you say to God, "I am exhausted and depressed beyond words, and I don't like You at all right now, and I recoil from most people who believe in You," that might be the most honest thing you've ever said. If you told me you had said to God, "It is all hopeless, and I don't have a clue if You exist, but I could use a hand," it would almost bring tears to my eyes, tears of pride in you, for the courage it takes to get real—really real. It would make me want to sit next to you at the dinner table.

So prayer is our sometimes real selves trying to communicate with the Real, with Truth, with the Light. It is us reaching out to be heard, hoping to be found by a light and warmth in the world, instead of darkness and cold. Even mushrooms respond to light—I suppose they blink their mushroomy little eyes, like the rest of us.

Light reveals us to ourselves, which is not always so great if you find yourself in a big disgusting mess, possibly of your own creation. But like sunflowers we turn toward light. Light warms, and in most cases it draws us to itself. And in this light, we can see beyond shadow and illusion to something beyond our modest receptors, to what is way beyond us, and deep inside.

This is all hard to articulate, because it is so real, so huge, beyond mystery. Rumi said that all words are fingers pointing to the moon, and we think the words are the moon. But because of the light, the light of love, the energy and motion that have called us to prayer, bits of this deeper reality are perceivable, and little bits of it will have to do.

My three prayers are variations on Help, Thanks, Wow. That's all I ever need, besides the silence, the pain, and the pause sufficient for me to stop, close my eyes, and turn inward.

HELP

It is all hopeless. Even for a crabby optimist like me, things couldn't be worse. Everywhere you turn, our lives and marriages and morale and government are falling to pieces. So many friends have broken children. The planet does not seem long for this world. Repent! Oh, wait, never mind. I meant: Help.

What I wanted my whole life was relief—from pressure, isolation, people's suffering (including my own, which was mainly mental), and entire political administrations. That is really all I want now. Besides dealing with standard-issue family crisis, heartbreak, and mishegas, I feel that I can't stand one single more death in my life. That's too bad, because as we speak, I have a cherished thirteen-year-old cat who is near death from lymphoma. I know I won't be able to live without her.

This must sound relatively petty to those of you facing the impending loss of people, careers, or retirement savings. But if you are madly in love with your pets, as any rational person is, you know what a loss it will be for both me and my three-year-old grandson, Jax. My cat Jeanie has helped raise him, and it will be his first death. I told him that she was sick, and that the angels were going to take her from us. I tried to make it sound like rather happy news—after all, vultures aren't coming for her, or snakes—but he wasn't having any of it.

"Angels are taking Jeanie away?"

Yes, because she is old and needs to go live in heaven now.

He said, "I'm mad at the angels." He's mad at death. I'm mad at death, too. I've had it. I am existentially sick to death of death, and I abso-lutely cannot stand that a couple of friends may lose their children. I cannot stand that my son's and grandson's lives will hold so much isola-tion, strife, death, and common yet humiliating

skin conditions. But as Kurt Vonnegut put it,
Welcome to the monkey house. This is a hard
planet, and we're a vulnerable species. And all
I can do is pray: Help.

When I pray, which I do many times a day,
I pray for a lot of things. I ask for health and
happiness for my friends, and for their children.
This is okay to do, to ask God to help them have a
sense of peace, and for them to feel the love of
God. I pray for our leaders to act in the common
good, or at least the common slightly better. I
pray that aid and comfort be rushed to people
after catastrophes, natural and man-made. It
is also okay to ask that my cat have an easy
death. Some of my friends' kids are broken and
the kids' parents are living in that, and other
friends' marriages are broken, and every family I love has serious problems involving someone's health or finances. But we can be big in
prayer, and trust that God won't mind if we pray
about the cat and Jax's tender heart.

Is God going to say, "Sorry, we don't have
enough for the cat"? I don't think so.

I ask for help for this planet, and for her poor,

and for the suffering people in my little galaxy. I know even as I pray for help that there will be tremendous compassion, mercy, generosity, companionship, and laughter from other people in the world, and from friends, doctors, nurses, hospice people. I also know that life can be devastating, and it's still okay to be pissed off at God: Mercy, schmercy. I always want the kid to live.

I can picture God saying: "Okay, hon. I'll be here when you're done with your list." Then He goes back to knitting new forests or helping less pissy people until I hit rock bottom. And when I finally do, there may be hope.

There's freedom in hitting bottom, in seeing that you won't be able to save or rescue your daughter, her spouse, his parents, or your career, relief in admitting you've reached the place of great unknowing. This is where restoration can begin, because when you're still in the state of trying to fix the unfixable, everything bad is engaged: the chatter of your mind, the tension of your physiology, all the trunks and wheel-ons you carry from the past. It's exhausting, crazy-making.

Help. Help us walk through this. Help us come through.

It is the first great prayer.

I don't pray for God to do this or that, or for God's sake to knock it off, or for specific outcomes. Well, okay, maybe a little. When my great hero Arthur Ashe had had AIDS for quite a while, he said: "God's will alone matters. When I played tennis, I never prayed for victory in a match. I will not pray now to be cured of heart disease or AIDS." So I pray, Help. Hold my friends in Your light.

There are no words for the broken hearts of people losing people, so I ask God, with me in tow, to respond to them with graciousness and encouragement enough for the day. Everyone we love and for whom we pray with such passion will die, which is the one real fly in the ointment, so we pray for miracles—please help this friend live, please help that friend die gracefully—and we pray for the survivors to somehow come through. Please help Joe survive Evelyn's dementia. Please help this town bounce back. Please help those parents come through, please help these kids come through. I pray to be able to bear my cat's loss. Help.

I try not to finagle God. Some days go better than others, especially during election years. I ask that God's will be done, and I mostly sort of mean it.

In prayer, I see the suffering bathed in light. In God, there is no darkness. I see God's light permeate them, soak into them, guide their feet. I *want* to tell God what to do: "Look, Pal, this is a catastrophe. You have *got* to shape up." But it wouldn't work. So I pray for people who are hurting, that they be filled with air and light. Air and light heal; they somehow get into those dark, musty places, like spiritual antibiotics.

We don't have to figure out how this all works—"Figure it out" is not a good slogan. It's enough to know it does.

There was so little air and light in my childhood, so little circulation and transparency and truth. When people and pets died, it was like the Big Eraser came and got them, except for a few mice and birds we buried in the backyard.

I was terrified of death by the time I was

three or four, actively if not lucidly. I had frequent nightmares about snakes and scary neighbors. By the age of four or five, I was terrified by my thoughts. By the time I was five, the migraines began. I was so sensitive about myself and the world that I cried or shriveled up at the slightest hurt. People always told me, "You've got to get a thicker skin," like now they might say, jovially, "Let go and let God." Believe me, if I could, I would, and in the meantime I feel like stabbing you in the forehead. Teachers wrote on my report cards that I was too sensitive, excessively worried, as if this were an easily correctable condition, as if I were wearing too much of the violet toilet water little girls wore then. At the same time, I didn't want to ask my parents for help, because they had so much on their hands. And besides, I *was* the helper. I was the go-to girl for everyone in my family. And ours wasn't a family who would ever, under almost any circumstances, ask others for help.

Plus, we didn't pray. I was raised to believe that people who prayed were ignorant. It was voodoo, asking an invisible old man to intervene, God as Santa Claus. God was the reason for most of the large-scale suffering in history, like the Crusades and the Inquisition. Therefore to pray was to throw your lot in with Genghis Khan and Torquemada (which was the name of our huge orange cat) and with snake handlers, instead of beautiful John Coltrane, William Blake, Billie Holiday. My parents worshipped at the church of *The New York Times*, and we bowed down before our antique hi-fi cabinet, which held the Ark of the Covenant—Miles Davis and Thelonious Monk albums.

So, to recap, my parents, who were too hip and intellectual to pray, worshipped mostly mentally ill junkies. Our best family friends drank and one-upped one another trashing common enemies, like Richard Nixon and Christians. I think it is safe to say that not one single family member or close family friend prayed, except for my paternal grandfather, who had been a Christian missionary and who loved his grandkids in a way he hadn't been able to love his kids. He had never once told my father that he loved him; that simply wasn't done. Almost all I remember of my grandfather is how bald and gentle he was. Also, that people in public were in awe of him. I remember sitting in his lap, and the smell of his pipe. I was six when he was erased.

I know beyond a shadow of a doubt, with no proof, that my grandfather prayed for all of us kids. And as it turns out, if one person is praying for you, buckle up. Things can happen.

The other day, my older brother, John, told me this story:

One night when he was seven and I was five, Mom and Dad went out and left us with our regular babysitter, a girl named Carol. When she went into the kitchen to heat up dinner, John recalled, I pulled him away from the TV. I told him urgently that I had to tell him a secret, but we had to be at the top of the stairs to the attic, and we couldn't be seen by Carol.

So as we huddled together at the top of the steps, I swore him to secrecy, and then said I wanted to take the baby Jesus into my heart.

He remembered that I was extremely agitated, and he could see that it was enormously important to me. I said, "We have to pray before they come home."

As soon as he told me this the other day, it all came back. I remember my tough brother and me bowing our heads and clasping our hands in prayer. Then the screen goes blank until my parents came home. John and I were in bed but still awake. I was scared to death that he would rat me out for praying, but he didn't. We got up and ran out to get hugs and kisses. I can still see the pajamas from Sears that I wore.

A few minutes later, Carol's father came to pick her up. I honestly do not remember Carol's having said anything to me about Jesus, but I do remember her father Charlie's hands. I had noticed them before because they were so different from my father's elegant writerly hands. Charlie's were huge and callused, and they were often injured, splintered or with a blue thumbnail where he'd hit it with a hammer. They were always dirty-looking, not because he didn't wash them but because his work, whatever it was, had indelibly ingrained the dirt into the calluses.

My brother thinks that they may have been

Mennonites. Carol must have said something to me that night, out of John's earshot; but maybe not. That is the first time I remember praying.

I have been praying on and off ever since, with a couple of bitter years as a teenage atheist when I discovered Bertrand Russell. I could always imagine God was near, or at least true.

And imagination is from God. It is part of the way we understand the world. I think it's okay to imagine God and grace the best you can. Some of the stuff we imagine engages and connects and calls for the very best in us to come out. Other imaginings disengage us, and shut us down. My understanding is that you get to choose which of your thoughts to go with.

Imagining God can be so different from wishful thinking, if your spiritual experiences change your behavior over time. Have you become more generous, which is the ultimate healing? Or more patient, which is a close second? Did your world become bigger and juicier and more tender? Have you become ever so slightly kinder to yourself? This is how you tell.

Help. A lifelong friend, a staunch agnostic, has asked me to pray for her daughter, Angie, who has young children and a diagnosis of aggressive lung cancer, the kind that continues to grow tumors in the midst of chemotherapy. I close my eyes and say in silence, "I hold this family in Your light. I pray for them to get their miracle, and to have stamina, for them to be okay today, for their love and amazing senses of humor to help them come through, although if You have a minute, I'd like to know: What on *earth* could You be thinking?"

That prayer and my friendship are pretty much all I've got to offer.

I wish I had a magic wand and could tap Angie on the head with it, and the cancer would be gone and her kids would get to grow up with a mother. Even better, I wish God had a magic wand. I've never seen evidence of it. But as I've written in various other places, I have seen miracles, although they always take too long to make themselves known, if you ask me. Also, I've seen grace manifest as spiritual WD-40, as water wings, as ribbons of fresh air in tight, scary rooms. And I've witnessed the intervention of goofy angels, the poor short-straw angels who seem to draw me.

I have seen many people survive unsurvivable losses, and seen them experience happiness again. How is this possible?

Love flowed to them from their closest people, and from their community, surrounded them, sat with them, held them, fed them, swept their floors. Time passed. In most cases, their pain evolved slowly into help for others. The great Bengali poet Rabindranath Tagore wrote, "I slept and dreamt that life was joy. / I awoke and saw that life was service. / I acted and behold, service was joy."

I know Angie and her mother will get a miracle, although it may not be the one they want—the one we pray for, in which the doctors break the grip of the cancer and help Angie live. But the family will come through, even if Angie dies. The little ones will need their grandma on board; time will pass. Death will not be the end of the story.

Human lives are hard, even those of health and privilege, and don't make much sense. This is the message of the Book of Job: Any snappy explanation of suffering you come up with will be horseshit. God tells Job, who wants an explanation for all his troubles, "You wouldn't understand."

And we don't understand a lot of things. But we learn that people are *very* disappointing, and that they break our hearts, and that very sweet people will be bullied, and that we *will* be called to survive unsurvivable losses, and that we will realize with enormous pain how much of our lives we've already wasted with obsessive work or pleasing people or dieting. We will see and read about deprivation and barbarity beyond our ability to understand, much less process. Side by side with all that, we will witness transformation, people finding out who they were born to be, before their parents pretzelized them into high achievers and addicts and charming, wired robots.

But where do we even start on the daily walk of restoration and awakening? We start where we are. We find God in our human lives, and that includes the suffering. I get thirsty people glasses of water, even if that thirsty person is just me. My friend Tom goes through the neighborhood and picks up litter, knowing there will be just as much tomorrow. We visit those shut-ins whom a higher power seems to have entrusted to our care—various relatives, often aging and possibly annoying, or stricken friends from our church communities, people in jails or mental institutions who might be related to us, who benefit from hearing our own resurrection stories. My personal belief is that God looks through Her Rolodex when She has a certain kind of desperate person in Her care, and assigns that person to some screwed-up soul like you or me, and makes it hard for us to ignore that person's suffering, so we show up even when it is extremely inconvenient or just *awful* to be there.

There is one problem with this system, which is that it may be necessary to leapfrog over almost everything you were taught about yourself. Possibly your parents were very much in love and had studied ways to love their kids as they were. And because of the robust mental health and harmony in which you were raised, you do not have a ton of baggage. Perhaps, because things were so stable and loving in your home, you did not have to learn survival skills of pretending not to see what was going on, or struggling to achieve perfection, or staying on your toes 24/7 in case Dad's mood went south or Mom started to get funny again and you needed to bolt.

But for the few of you who were not raised that way, you may need to play along with me here and act as if it would be okay with your families to break the contract and tell the truth and have—and voice—scary feelings. And then renounce *The New York Times* and your bank account as the golden calves of your life, to instead imagine and act on the idea that there is a power greater than yourself.

But what if you just can't, even in desperate fear? I would lend you my higher power, this sweet brown-eyed Jew who will want you to get glasses of water for everyone, and then come to the beach for some nice fish.

Or maybe you have a crack in your disbelief.

As many great sages have said, that's how the light gets in. What if I asked you to suspend your conviction just for a few minutes, and pretend there is someone outside you who hears you if you pray?

Thirty years ago I suggested to a famously atheistic San Francisco artist, who was dying of alcoholism, that as an experiment he *act* as if he had a higher power in his life. He loved this, and got six weeks of great happiness at the end of his days, having conversations with what he called his great HP—and later his great Hewlett-Packard. I saw him every other day: he was radiant. Friends visited frequently, and took him for drives in the country, on ferryboat rides, and to lunch at Enrico's. Then he started to drink again, became mean and ugly and fiercely atheistic, and died after driving all of us away, true to his beliefs till the end.

If I were going to begin practicing the presence of God for the first time today, it would help to begin by admitting the three most terrible truths of our existence: that we are so ruined, and so loved, and in charge of so little. Of course it wasn't our fault that we ended up so ruined or felt so undeserving of love, and that if people knew our true selves better or if our minds had PA systems, they would run for their cute little lives. Can you imagine that you have a true self, way down deep inside, a self that will still be there even if your mind goes?

If you can imagine that, it's not such a huge step to imagine yourself believing in any sort of higher power, to whom you could say, "Hey."

I had a great friend named Jack, who has since passed, who was all but destroyed by the Catholic Church. So when he began a new, sober life, he turned in prayer to our local mountain, Tamalpais, the sleeping Indian maiden whom the coastal Miwok worshipped. I love the memory of this plump salesman from St. Louis worshipping a sacred mountain, beseeching and praising and turning to God in Her distressing guise as a forested landmass.

I have a brilliant friend with a master's degree who experiences God as a low-seated easy chair whose arms are very long and upholstered and actually hold her. I know a person with a

Ph.D. who goes to a church based on Star Wars: May the force be with you.

But you know what? When he and my other friends and I have run out of good ideas on how to fix the unfixable, when we finally stop trying to heal our own sick, stressed minds with our sick, stressed minds, when we are truly at the end of our rope and just done, we say the same prayer.

We say, "Help."

We say, Help, this is really all too much, or I am going slowly crazy, or I can't do this, or I can't *stop* doing this, or I can't feel anything. Or, Help, he is going to leave me, or I have no life, or I hate the one I've created, or I forgot to have a life, or I forgot to pay attention as it scrolled by. Or even, Help, I hate her so much, and one of my parents is dying—or will never die. Unfortunately, we haven't even gotten to the big-ticket items yet: cancer, financial ruin, lost children, incontinence.

And me? Now it turns out that my cat is going to die later today. She is struggling to breathe. I had hoped and prayed that she would slip off in the night and that I would not have to have the vet come by to put her down. I said, Help. Also, I gave her a lot of morphine, what *had* to have been an overdose, which she just slept off. All I wanted was for her not to die miserable and afraid. That's all.

It is nighttime now, and Jeanie passed an hour ago, miserable and afraid.

When the vet came, we tried to gently get her out from under the futon, and she went crazy, and the next ten minutes were so awful that I won't describe them. Suffice it to say that she did not go gently into that good night. It broke my heart. But she had been suffering, and is suffering no more. She had an amazing run of love with my family. She was a proud little union cat, and also a model of queenly disdain with a bit of grudging affection for most people, and pure adoration for me.

Was my prayer answered? Yes, although I didn't get what I'd hoped and prayed for, what I'd selected from the menu. Am I sick with anxi-

ety, that I did the wrong thing? Of course. Sad?
Heartbroken. But Jeanie hit the lottery when
she got me as her person for thirteen years, and
the bad death was only ten minutes. So let me
get back to you on this.

There are a lot of prayers in the world, some of
them better known than others. The Serenity
Prayer is one of the most famous institution-
alized prayers of the world, a Greatest Hits
prayer. The best-known version says: "God,
grant me the serenity to accept the things I
cannot change, the courage to change the things
I can, and the wisdom to know the difference."
There's a slightly comic version—"God, grant
me the serenity to accept the things I cannot
change, the courage to change the things I can,
and the weaponry to make the difference"—
but let's stick to the first. A sober friend from
Texas said once that the three things I cannot change are the past, the truth, and you. I
hate this insight so much. My experience is that

when I use this prayer to God, I am at the same time alerting the person inside me that I need to rein myself. It is a reset button prayer. In certain ways it serves the same function that sitting down at my desk at the same time every day does for my creative self: it alerts my subconscious to the fact that it is time for it to kick in. It looks at its little watch and says, "Oh, for God's sake, is it nine o'clock already?" It is prayer as memo to self.

By the time my mother's Alzheimer's had progressed to the point where my brothers and I had to take her out of her assisted-living apartment, where she had declined in the cherished company of a truly awful Himalayan cat named Baby, I had been praying sort of hostilely to God for a while: "Could You let her die in her own bed, in the night, with Baby beside her? And then take fat Baby out with a stroke? This would kill You?"

In the end I was reduced to beggy prayers: "Please don't make me have to take the cat out of her arms. . . . If You could just do this *one* thing and not make me take the cat out of her arms." But one day I had to. It was time. I prayed,

"Help. Enter this mess." And I lied to my mother. She was sitting in her wheelchair, beaming at me. I told her that her doctor, whom she adored, wanted her to go for physical therapy for a week or two, until her balance was better. And I took the cat out of her arms. I said enthusiastically, "See you in a week, Baby."

My mom needed to be in a nursing home. That was her reality. The cat could not come with her. Did it suck? Yes. Was my prayer— Help—answered? Was it excruciating? Yes. Did my mother end up in a warm, gentle place with nice light and nurses and exquisite care, where her closest people could visit and comfort her, make her laugh, kiss her, read to her, and bring her delicious treats? Yes. Is it less of a beautiful prayer experience because it involved lying? Not to me.

There is Thomas Merton's famous prayer, the beginning of which reads, "My Lord God, I have no idea where I am going. I do not see the road ahead of me." You can look up the rest.

There is a beautiful prayer a friend's Jewish mother wrote and taught me, which I swear by:

Help for the sick and hungry,

home for the homeless folk,

peace in the world forever.

this is my prayer, O Lord. Amen.

I wrote one that will do in a pinch:

Hi, God.

I am just a mess.

It is all hopeless.

What else is new?

I would be sick of me, if I were You, but
*   miraculously You are not.*

I know I have no control over other people's
*   lives, and I hate this. Yet I believe that if I*
*   accept this and surrender, You will meet me*
*   wherever I am.*

Wow. Can this be true? If so, how is this
*   afternoon—say, two-ish?*

Thank You in advance for Your company and
*   blessings.*

You have never once let me down.

Amen.

A certain priest friend of mine who spends
too much time in the Old Testament says that *all*

prayers should include the hope that the children of one's enemies end up living in the
streets.

But beautiful pre-assembled prayers—like
the Merton, the Lord's Prayer, the Twenty-third
Psalm—have saved me more times than I can remember. But they are for special occasions. They
are dressier prayers, the good china of prayers,
used when I have my wits about me enough
(a) to remember that they exist, and (b) to get
into a state of trust. This would be approximately
seven percent of the time.

Most good, honest prayers remind me that I
am not in charge, that I cannot fix anything, and
that I open myself to being helped by something,
some force, some friends, some *something*.
These prayers say, "Dear Some Something, I
don't know what I'm doing. I can't see where I'm
going. I'm getting more lost, more afraid, more
clenched. Help."

These prayers acknowledge that I am clue-
less; but something else isn't. While I am not
going to go limp, I am asking for the willingness
to step into truth. It's like the old riddle: What's

the difference between you and God? God never thinks he's you.

One modest tool for letting go in prayer that I've used for twenty-five years is a God box. I've relied on every imaginable container—from a pillbox, to my car's glove box, to decorative boxes friends have given me. The container has to exist in time and space, so you can physically put a note into it, so you can *see* yourself let go, in time and space.

On a note, I write down the name of the person about whom I am so distressed or angry, or describe the situation that is killing me, with which I am so toxically, crazily obsessed, and I fold the note up, stick it in the box and close it. You might have a brief moment of prayer, and it might come out sounding like this: "Here. You think you're so big? Fine. You deal with it. Although I have a few more excellent ideas on how best to proceed." Then I agree to keep my sticky mitts off the spaceship until I hear back.

The willingness to do such a childish thing comes from the pain of not being able to let go of something. The willingness comes from finding yourself half mad with obsession. We learn through pain that some of the things we thought were castles turn out to be prisons, and we desperately want out, but even though we built them, we can't find the door. Yet maybe if you ask God for help in knowing which direction to face, you'll have a moment of intuition. Maybe you'll see at least one next right step you can take.

The response probably won't be from God, in the sense of hearing a deep grandfatherly voice, or via skywriting, or in the form of an LED-lit airplane aisle at your feet. But the mail will come, or an e-mail, or the phone will ring; unfortunately, it might not be later today, ideally right after lunch, but you will hear back. You will come to know.

When we think we can do it all ourselves—fix, save, buy, or date a nice solution—it's hopeless. We're going to screw things up. We're going to get our tentacles wrapped around things and squirt our squiddy ink all over, so that there is even less visibility, and then we're going to squeeze the very life out of everything.

Or we can summon a child's courage and

faith and put a note with a few words into a small box in the hope that we can get our sucking, inky squid tentacles off things.

We do this without a clue about what will happen, how it will all turn out. You may be saying: "It's so awful right now, and I am so pissed off and sad and mental, that against all odds I'm giving up. I'll accept whatever happens."

Maybe after you put a note in the God box, you'll go a little limp, and in that divine limpness you'll be able to breathe again. Then you're halfway home. In many cases, breath is all you need. Breath is holy spirit. Breath is Life. It's oxygen. Breath might get you a little rest. You must be *so* exhausted.

With a God box, you're finally announcing to the universe that you can't do it, that you have ruined things enough for the time being. Imagine the burlesque look of surprise on the universe's face! The great cosmic double-take; then a fist pump.

This is what gets everyone off the hook, the hook being the single worst place to be. My priest friend Bill Rankin said that through prayer, we take ourselves off the hook and put God on the hook, where God belongs. When you're on the hook, you're thrashing, helpless, furious, like a smaller kid lifted by the seat of his pants by a mean big kid. Jesus, on the literal hook of the cross, says to God, "Help," and God enters into every second of the Passion like a labor nurse.

When you get your hooks out of something, it can roll away, down its own hill, away from you. It can breathe again. It got away from you, and your tight, sweaty grip, and your stagnant dog breath, the torture of watching you do somersaults and listening to you whine "What if?" and "Wait, wait, I have ONE more idea. . . ."

You can go from monkey island, with endless chatter, umbrage, and poop-throwing, to *what is happening right in front of me*. God, what a concept. It means I stop trying to figure it out, because trying to figure it out is exhausting and crazy-making. Doping it out has become the problem.

So when we cry out Help, or whisper it into our chests, we enter the paradox of not going limp and not feeling so hopeless that we can barely walk, and we release ourselves from the absolute craziness of trying to be our own—or other people's—higher powers.

Help.

We can be freed from a damaging insistence on forward thrust, from a commitment to running wildly down a convenient path that might actually be taking us deeper into the dark forest. Praying "Help" means that we ask that Something give us the courage to stop in our tracks, right where we are, and turn our fixation away from the Gordian knot of our problems. We stop the toxic peering and instead turn our eyes to something else: to our feet on the sidewalk, to the middle distance, to the hills, whence our help comes—someplace else, anything else. Maybe this is a shift of only eight degrees, but it can be a miracle.

It may be one of those miracles where your heart sinks, because you think it means you have lost. But in surrender you have won. And if it were me, after a moment, I would say, Thanks.

THANKS

Thanks" is the short form of the original prayer I used to say in gratitude for any unexpected grace in my life, "Thankyouthankyouthankyou." As I grew spiritually, the prayer became the more formal "Thank you," and now, from the wrinkly peaks of maturity, it is simply "Thanks."

Now as then, most of the time for me gratitude is a rush of relief that I dodged a bullet—the highway patrol guy didn't notice me speed by, or the dog didn't get hit by someone else speeding by. Or "Oh my God, thankyouthankyouthankyou" that it was all a dream, my child didn't drown, I didn't pick up a drink or appear on *Oprah* in underpants with my dreadlocks dropping off my head. These are all DEFCON 1

moments of relief and gratitude worth giving
God thanks.

The second and third levels of the second
great prayer are said with a heaving exhalation
of breath, the expulsion of bellows—THANK
you, whoooooosh. The constables found my
passport. The brakes held. The proliferation of
white blood cells was about allergies, not leuke-
mia; the pediatrician canceled the appointment
with the head of oncology and instead recom-
mended Benadryl. Oh my God: thanks.

How can you help saying thank you after
moments like these, when real danger is
averted? Even atheists do. Agnostics joke, "The
man upstairs must like me," as if it's the dean
of admissions. I personally clutch at my chest
and cry, "Thanks, my God, thanks," and at such
moments I would kneel and press my forehead
to the ground if my right knee would not begin
to sob. Then I usually move to: "I owe You big
this time, I'll never ask for anything else. This
time I mean it."

It is easy to thank God for life when things
are going well. But life is much bigger than we

give it credit for, and much of the time it's harder
than we would like. It's a package deal, though.
Sometimes our mouths sag open with exhaus-
tion, and our souls and minds do, too, with de-
feat, and that saggy opening is what we needed
all along. Any opening leads to the chance of
flow, which sometimes is the best we can hope
for, and a minor miracle at that, open and fasci-
nated, instead of tense and scared and shut
down. God, thank you.

We and life are spectacularly flawed and
complex. Often we do not get our way, which
I hate, hate, hate. But in my saner moments
I remember that if we did, usually we would
shortchange ourselves. Sometimes circumstances conspire to remind us or even let us
glimpse how thin the membrane is between here
and there, between birth and the grave, between the human and the divine. In wonder at
the occasional direct experience of this, we say,
Thank you.

I thank God when my obsessive looping
is alleviated. Oh, God, thank you—ten whole
minutes just passed without one thought of a

cigarette or a drink or the horrible ex. I got through the bad appointment with my doctor, my bank, my lawyer: the worst is over. (Actually, under no circumstances should you ever say or even think that the worst is over. You will bring the evil eye down on yourself so fast it will leave you keening. But it is okay to say, "That could have been so much worse," which is always the case.)

Gratitude runs the gamut from shaking your head and saying, "Thanks, wow, I appreciate it so much," for your continued health, or a good day at work, or the first blooms of the daisies in the public park, to saying, "Thanks, that's a re-lief," when it's not the transmission, or an abscess, or an audit notice from the IRS. "Thanks" can be the recognition that you have been blessed mildly, or with a feeling as intense as despair at the miracle of having been spared. You say Thankyouthankyouthankyouthankyou: My wife is going to live. We get to stay in this house. They found my son: he's in jail, but he's alive; we know where he is and he's safe for the night.

Things could have gone either way, but they came down on our side. It could have been much, much worse, and it wasn't. Heads, we won.

And of course, gratitude can be for everything in between, from the daily break of good luck and found money, to the magical, mystical magnetic force of quiet or exuberant relief, when you know that something—God, fate, luck, kismet, the law, Powerball—has smiled on you big-time.

Domestic pain can be searing, and it is usually what does us in. It's almost indigestible: death, divorce, old age, drugs; brain-damaged children, violence, senility, unfaithfulness. Good luck with figuring it out. It unfolds, and you experience it, and it is so horrible and endless that you could almost give up a dozen times. But grace can be the experience of a second wind, when even though what you want is clarity and resolution, what you get is stamina and poignancy and the strength to hang on. Through the most ordinary things, books, for instance, or a postcard, or eyes or hands, life is transformed. Hands that for decades reached out to

hurt us, to drag us down, to control us, or to
wave us away in dismissal now reach for us
differently. They become instruments of tender-
ness, buoyancy, exploration, hope.

We sing a slow hymn at my church, St.
Andrew, that goes, "God has smiled on me, He
has set me free." For us to acknowledge that we
have been set free from toxic dependency, from
crippling obsession or guilt, that we have been
graced with the ability finally to forgive someone, is just plain astonishing. You can't have
gotten from where you were—gripped by anxi-
ety, tiny with fear—to come through to freedom,
for God's sake. To have been so lost that you
felt abducted, to feeling found, returned, and set
back onto your feet: Oh my God, thankyouthankyouthankyou. Thank you. Thanks.

A lot of us religious types go around saying
thank you to God when we find a good parking space, or locate the house keys or the wan-
dering phone, or finally get a good night's

sleep. And while that may be annoying to the people around us, it's important because if we are lucky, gratitude becomes a habit. You say "Thank you" when something scary has happened in your beloved and screwed-up family and you all came through (or most of you did), and you have found love in the intergenerational ruins (maybe a lot of love, or maybe just enough). Or you can look at what was revealed in the latest mess, and you say thanks for the revelation, because it shows you some truth you needed to know, and that can be so rare in our families, let alone in our culture, our world, and in our marriages, and in our relationships with our teenagers and with ourselves.

You say, Thank you for lifting this corner of the curtain so I can see the truth, maybe for just a moment, but in a way that might change my life forever. And that moment is astonishing, because everything is taking place all at once, the micro and the macro. You walk through the glittering city and gaze up at the heavens, and yet down here you can see clearly what you have on your hands, or even what you have lost.

Most of us figure out by a certain age—some of us later than others—that life unspools in cycles, some lovely, some painful, but in no predictable order. So you could have lovely, painful, and painful again, which I think we all agree is not at all fair. You don't have to like it, and you are always welcome to file a brief with the Complaints Department. But if you've been around for a while, you know that much of the time, if you are patient and are paying attention, you will see that God will restore what the locusts have taken away.

I admit, sometimes this position of gratitude can be a bit of a stretch. So many bad things happen in each of our lives. Who knew? When my son, Sam, was seven and discovered that he and I would probably not die at exactly the same moment, he began to weep and said, "If I had known that, I wouldn't have agreed to be born." This one truth, that the few people you adore will die, is plenty difficult to absorb. But on top of it, someone's brakes fail, or someone pulls the trigger or snatches the kid, or someone deeply trusted succumbs to temptation, and everything falls apart. We are hurt beyond any reasonable chance of healing. We are haunted by our failures and mortality. And yet the world keeps on spinning, and in our grief, rage, and fear a few people keep on loving us and showing up. It's all motion and stasis, change and stagnation. Awful stuff happens and beautiful stuff happens, and it's all part of the big picture.

In the face of everything, we slowly come through. We manage to make new constructs and baskets to hold what remains, and what has newly appeared. We come to know—or reconnect with—something rich and okay about ourselves. And at some point, we cast our eyes to the beautiful skies, above all the crap we're wallowing in, and we whisper, "Thank you."

When someone shares with you a horrible truth—about the marriage that seemed fine, or work that seemed valuable, or a mind that turned out to be weaker than you thought—you say, "Thank you for the openness between us—that's the greatest gift." When someone you love can reframe something that was excruciating—having at last faced putting her husband in a home, or having watched her book or hopes or retirement account sink—and genuinely see something blessed in the mess, you say thank you. You say "Thank you" that in the revelation, whether it's ordinary or difficult, this person you love has found a way to the balm of gratitude. What a relief.

Revelation is not for the faint at heart. Some of us with tiny paranoia issues think that so much information and understanding is being withheld from us—by colleagues, by family, by life, by God—knowledge that would save us, and help us break the code and enable us to experience life with peace and amusement. But in our quieter moments we remember that (a) there are no codes, and (b) if you are paying attention, plenty is being revealed. We are too often distracted by the need to burnish our surfaces, to look good so that other people won't know what screwed-up messes we, or our mate or kids or finances, are. But if you gently help yourself back to the present moment, you see how life keeps stumbling along and how you may actually find your way through another ordinary or impossible day. Details are being revealed, and they will take you out of yourself, which is heaven, and you will have a story to tell, which is salvation that again and again saves us, the way Jesus saves some people, or the way sobriety does. Stories to tell or hear—either way, it's medicine. The Word.

So I say "Thanks," because revelation has shown me things that are miserable that somehow I may get to sidestep; or that are miserable but that prayer and friends help me find a way through; or that are painful and beautiful in ways that make your heart ache, that draw you closer forever to the comrades who have walked with you.

Without revelation and reframing, life can seem like an endless desert of danger with scratchy sand in your shoes, and yet if we remember or are reminded to pay attention, we find so many sources of hidden water, so many bits and chips and washes of color, in a weed or the gravel or a sunrise. There are so many ways to sweep the sand off our feet. So we say, "Oh my God. Thanks."

My pastor Veronica says that God always makes a way out of no way. This means that at some point, often against all odds, we will say "Thanks." Now, Veronica is paid to have faith, but even I—who am not paid to have faith— know that this is true. I don't always believe it, but I know it is true.

Recently I was going to meet my great and amazing friends Barbara and Susie for a walk, or rather, a stroll and roll, as Barbara has Lou Gehrig's disease. As I have pointed out to her, Lou Gehrig's is the one disease you are supposed to actively try to avoid. But she went ahead and got a full-blown case, which has come to mean she uses a walker, feeding tubes, and a computerized speaking device called Kate that works through her iPad. So Susie drove us to see the Pacific Ocean from above San Francisco's Moraga steps. I had not yet settled down into what is true—that Barbara is pretty sick and getting worse—so I sat in a state of jovial nervousness in the backseat, feeling alone and useless and superficial. When we arrived, the view was socked in with fog. We gamely got out of the

car anyway, and on top of everything—the
Lou Gehrig's, the vichyssoise fog, my anxious
sorrow—there was one of those mean winds
that prick at your body and your mind and your
very being. Plus, they make your skin look terrible. Just ghastly.

It was all hopeless. I had no choice but to
pray. This is all a mess, I said to God. I love these
two women so much, and I had had such high
hopes for connection and joy today: Help.

And I got my divine revelation: We all
needed to get back into the car, immediately.
This took a while, as there is not much immediately when you're with someone who has ALS.
But at some point, warmth and golden sun
flooded through the car windows, and Susie
drove us around the neighborhood, and from
inside we took in the brilliant gardens of suc-
culents and crazy bright splashy exotic petals.
We found the one perfect parking spot at the
foot of the steps, where we could spend as much
time as we liked looking up directly at the magical mosaic on the tall, steep steps: at the bottom,
random plump fish in nursery colors swim

against the deep blue of the sea, and then come creatures that are beneath the ground, spiraling to animals that walk on the earth, and then to what is above, to the sky, and birds, and clouds, and an exuberant Mexican sun, which curls up into the expansiveness of a starry, starry night.

We all got so happy. We talked about real things for an hour: life, death, families, feeding tubes, faith. I asked Barbara, who does not eat food anymore, "What are you most grateful for these days?" She typed on her iPad, and Kate's mechanical voice spoke for her: "The beauty of nature, the birds and flowers, the beauty of friends."

This is called radical gratitude in the face of whatever life throws at you.

I was so glad and so grateful to be there with them that day—euphoric.

Gratitude begins in our hearts and then dovetails into behavior. It almost always makes you willing to be of service, which is where the joy resides. It means you are willing to stop being such a jerk. When you are aware of all that has been given to you, in your lifetime and in the past few days, it is hard not to be humbled, and pleased to give back.

Most humbling of all is to comprehend the lifesaving gift that your pit crew of people has been for you, and all the experiences you have shared, the journeys together, the collaborations, births and deaths, divorces, rehab, and vacations, the solidarity you have shown one another. Every so often you realize that without all of them, your life would be barren and pathetic. It would be *Death of a Salesman*, though with e-mail and texting.

The marvel is only partly that somehow you lured them into your web twenty years ago, forty years ago, and they totally stuck with you. The more astonishing thing is that these greatest of all possible people feel the same way about you—horrible, grim, self-obsessed you. They say—or maybe I said—that a good marriage is one in which each spouse secretly thinks he or she got the better deal, and this is true also of our bosom friendships. You could almost flush with appreciation. What a great scam, to have gotten people of such extreme quality and loyalty to think you are stuck with them. Oh my God. Thank you.

The truth is that "to whomever much is given, of him will much be required; and to whom much was entrusted, of him more will be asked," if Jesus is to be believed. He meant us, not the Kennedys or the Romneys—us, to whom such exquisite companions have been given. In the face of this, we mysteriously find ourselves willing to pick up litter in the street, or let others go first in traffic. Or even to let the psychotic talk to us for longer than a normal person would, to set aside the apprehension or boredom we feel and actually listen.

Father Gregory Boyle, the Jesuit who founded Homeboy Industries, a program that helps former gang members reenter society, reminds us that gratitude is not about waving your arms in praise on Christian TV shows. That's what we think God would want, because we would *love* to have a few hundred people applauding us, waving their arms like palm fronds.

Instead, God's idea of a good time is to see us picking up litter. God must love to see us serving food at the soup kitchen at Glide Memorial Church, or hear us calling our meth-head cousin just to check in because no one else in the family speaks to him. He can be long-winded and a handful, but we used to put each other's peas in the glasses of root beer at holiday dinners, so we have history together. With two other cousins we took naps together in one big bed. So we pick up the two-hundred-pound phone, dial his number, and say, "How are you?"

I really believe that God's idea of a good time is also to see us sharing what we have worked so hard to have, or to see us flirting with the old guy in line at the health food store, telling him our grandfather had a hat just like his, even though that is a lie.

When you have been able to cry out "Thank you" upon finding your lost child at the mall, or for getting off booze, it can naturally make you willing to take time with the homeless (although you are in a hurry and do not approve, and your rigid little right-wing friends have tried to convince you that the destitute are making more money than working people by standing at the intersection of Van Ness and Geary with their signs and cups and dirty children).

Is it okay yet to love and admire Mother Teresa again? Can we forget her detractors for long enough to remember that most mornings she was out there on the streets of Calcutta cleaning some person's butt the day before he died, without telling anyone about it?

"Thanks" is a huge mind-shift, from thinking that God wants our happy chatter and a public demonstration and is deeply interested in our opinions of the people we hate, to feeling quiet gratitude, humbly and amazingly, without shame at having been so blessed.

You breathe in gratitude, and you breathe it out, too. Once you learn how to do that, then you can bear someone who is unbearable. My general-purpose go-to mystic Rumi said, "There are hundreds of ways to kneel and kiss the ground," and bearing the barely bearable is one of the best.

When we go from rashy and clenched to grateful, we sometimes get to note the experience of grace, in knowing that we could not have gotten ourselves from where we were stuck, in hate or self-righteousness or self-loathing (which are the same thing), to freedom. The movement of grace in our lives toward freedom is the mystery. So we simply say "Thanks." Something had to open, something had to give, and I don't have a clue how to get things to do that. But they did, or grace did.

Thank you.

Frequently, as so many poets and psalmists and songwriters have said, the invisible shift happens through the broken places. It might be through financial failure, or a divorce, or an emotional train wreck instead of winning the Nobel Prize, which I would prefer: "This year's Nobel Prize in humility goes to . . ."

Being at our least grateful, our pissiest and

most self-obsessed, may create enough pain that we remember to do the footwork, get out of the house, or reach for the phone, or to get on our knees, or to get the hell outside. We ask for help. We call the horrible mentor, or the sweetest confidante, or even our meth-head cousin, who picks up and then can't talk—thank you, Jesus—because he thinks snakes have gotten into his car's dashboard, behind the radio, which is one of the occupational hazards of living in downtown San Francisco—all the radio snakes. And yet we get full credit for making the call. Having done the right thing lifts us out of the glop, the dregs of our own delusional thinking, and puts us a bit closer to being on the right track.

Saying and meaning "Thanks" leads to a crazy thought: What more can I give? We take the action first, by giving—and then the insight follows, that this fills us. Sin is not the adult bookstore on the corner. It is the hard heart, the lack of generosity, and all the isms, racism and sexism and so forth. But is there a crack where a ribbon of light might get in, might sneak past all the roadblocks and piles of stones, mental and emotional and cultural?

We can't will ourselves to be more generous and accepting. Most of us are more like the townspeople of Shirley Jackson's "The Lottery" than we are like the Dalai Lama. I know I am. And this is what hell is like.

It obviously behooves me to practice being receptive, open for the business of gratitude.

A nun I know once told me she kept begging God to take her character defects away from her. After years of this prayer, God finally got back to her: I'm not going to take anything away from you, you have to give it to Me.

I have found that I even have to pray for the willingness to give up the stuff I hate most about myself. I have to ask for help, and sometimes beg. That's the human condition. I just love my own guck so much. Help. Then I try to be a good person, a better person than I was yesterday, or an hour ago. In general, the Ten Commandments are not a bad place to start, nor is the Golden Rule. We try not to lie so much or kill anyone that day. We do the footwork, which comes down mostly to paying attention and trying not to be such a jerk. We try not to feel and act so entitled. We let others go first.

How can something so simple be so profound, letting others go first, in traffic or in line at Starbucks, and even if no one cares or notices? Because for the most part, people won't care—they're late, they haven't heard back from their new boyfriend, or they're fixated on the stock market. And they won't notice that you let them go ahead of you.

They take it as their due.

But you'll know. And it can change your whole day, which could be a way to change your whole life. There really is only today, although luckily that is also the eternal now. And maybe one person in the car in the lane next to you or in line at the bank or at your kid's baseball game will notice your casual generosity and will be touched, lifted, encouraged—in other words, slightly changed for the better—and later will let someone else go first. And this will be quantum.

The movement of grace toward gratitude brings us from the package of self-obsessed madness to a spiritual awakening. Gratitude is peace. Maybe you won't always get from being a brat to noticing that it is an e. e. cummings morning out the window. But some days you will. You will go from being Doug or Wendy Whiner, with your psychic diverticulitis, able to eat only macaroni and cheese, to remembering "i thank You God for most this amazing / day." You splurge on a pint basket of figs, or a pair of great socks. You begin to feel friendship with your flowering pear tree, an interspecies oneness with it, although we usually keep these thoughts to ourselves, lest they be used against us at the commitment hearings. In fact, you are able to use the word "wonder" again, even feel it, without despair that the New York literati or your atheist friends will find out and send you into exile.

This morning at six when I awoke, loneliness was sitting on my chest like a dental X-ray apron, even though I was buried in hairy dog love. I prayed: "Help. I am sad and lonely, and already it looks from here like today is going to be too long." So I did a kindness to myself, as I would have if a troubled friend had confided her lone-liness to me: I heated up the milk for my coffee. Then I took the dogs for a short hike in the hills. My girl Lily is getting quite old, and while she is going to live forever, we have to go for shorter walks now. They are not manic-Annie exercise walks anymore—about this I am bitter—where I burn off three hundred calories and get to feel morally superior and eat more all day. They are half as long, and slower, more amble than power walk, but of course they are lovely still.

We hiked in the northern foothills of Mount Tamalpais, which lay stretched out above us, serene and curvaceous, sloping down to the sea. I can remember taking hikes up here with Sam and Lily when we first got her, a big rescue puppy encrusted with ticks. As she grew up, she'd still tear around for a while, but then she'd pause to stare nobly out at the vista like a dog in the movies—Lassie maybe, or Benji at his most Harrison Ford. Lily was limping when we arrived here today, more Amahl and the Night Visitors than Lassie. And instead of gentle warmth to soothe her joints, there was a wind.

Another damn wind. I hate wind so much. It can make you feel hopeless, even in world-class beauty.

So I prayed: "Help me not be such an ass." (This is actually the fourth great prayer, which perhaps we will address at another time.)

After a few minutes, I noticed something: Because of the wind, the view was free of particulates in the air, and was so sharp and clear that it looked like one of those crisply bad paintings that are too true-to-life. After a few minutes the wind had blown away much of my unhappiness, and it actually made me laugh, that our green fleecy hills, like torsos in repose, managed to look like a nineteenth-century French painting. Wonderful!

The scent of spring was as light as goodness, pure and natural, mixed with the smells of mulch and grass and the old-lady perfume of wildflowers. This smell means baseball to me. I looked across the wooded canyon at Mount

Tamalpais and shouted, "Thank you, Mother," and would not have cared if someone had come along and heard me. As it turned out, no one did, and I sat down with the dogs. The landscape was bare in the wind. A lot of birds were grounded. I sat in the dirt for so long that the dogs fell asleep on the warm carpet of earth.

68

WOW

The third great prayer, Wow, is often offered with a gasp, a sharp intake of breath, when we can't think of another way to capture the sight of shocking beauty or destruction, of a sudden unbidden insight or an unexpected flash of grace. "Wow" means we are not dulled to wonder. We click into being fully present when we're stunned into that gasp, by the sight of a birth, or images of the World Trade Center towers falling, or the experience of being in a fjord, at dawn, for the first time. "Wow" is about having one's mind blown by the mesmerizing or the miraculous: the veins in a leaf, birdsong, volcanoes.

Many people believe the word comes from

the Scottish language: Robert Burns used it in a poem in 1791, "Tam o' Shanter": "An', wow! Tam saw an unco sight!" ("Unco" means strange and unfamiliar, which you probably knew.) You exclaim "Wow" upon first tasting halvah, and upon first hearing that the Scottish not only *eat* haggis but *love* haggis.

Wow is the child seeing the ocean for the first time. Wow is the teenager's Christmas car (secondhand, but still). Wow is John Muir, Walt Whitman, Mary Oliver saying that the sun was the "best preacher that ever was."

The word "wow" is found in Child's collection of early ballads:

> But bye and ryde the Black Douglas,
> And wow but he was rough!
> For he pulld up the bonny brier
> And flang't in St Mary's Loch.

I know that guy—we went out briefly and I am still getting over it. Any little thing would set off a new round of flanging.

Some etymologists think "wow" is a contraction of "I vow," the short form of "Holy Glasgow. I'vow!" This theory sounds right to me.

I remember hearing "Wow" for the first time from the mouth of our most beloved family friend, a German nature-lover named Gertrud. She said "Vow!" a lot when she and her husband took my family out onto San Francisco Bay on their small sailboat, and when we went on a wildflower hike in Yosemite. "Vow, look at this," looking straight up from beneath the Golden Gate Bridge. "Vow! Look at zis!" Alpine blue spider lupine, monkeyflowers, paintbrush. Wow, because you are almost speechless, but not quite.

You can manage, barely, this one syllable.

When we are stunned to the place beyond words, we're finally starting to get somewhere. It is so much more comfortable to think that we know what it all means, what to expect and how it all hangs together. When we are stunned to the place beyond words, when an aspect of life takes us away from being able to chip away at something until it's down to a manageable size and then to file it nicely away, when all we can say in response is "Wow," that's a prayer.

Wows come in all shapes and sizes, like people. There are the lowercase wows. These are the times when we sink into something modest that delivers above and beyond. When you crawl between clean sheets after a hard day, you are saved. You feel like you are the best sandwich ever. You're being taken care of from the top and the bottom, with not a crumb or a lump or a wrinkle. Wow: you can't believe you felt so low and lonely till you thought to change the sheets.

The cotton feels like cool smooth skin.

A lowercase wow might be seeing a kid execute a dive at the town pool, or coming upon a blanket of poppies in the field that was destroyed by grass fire last summer.

And then there are the uppercase Wows. Yosemite. Fireworks. Watching puppies being born at the neighbors' when you were six. Remember first semi-sort-of being able to imagine the sheer size of dinosaurs, at five or six, trying to comprehend how a brontosaurus could be seventy-five feet long? And what those feet must have looked like? As you studied dinosaurs in school or in a book you took out from the library because you *had* to know more about them, you learned that they were doomed and that they died out. And you saw paintings of them with their dinosaur families, and you saw that they did wriggly, pouncy, family stuff, the nicer ones nibbling on high leaves, like gigantic lumpy giraffes or like your grandfather taking a piece of turkey before Thanksgiving dinner. Then they were gone—kaput. When you're a little kid, that's about as trippy as science gets: These huge creatures once roamed the earth, and now are fossils; everything, from stegosaurus to your granddad, appears, roams the earth for a little while, and then vanishes. Wow.

And let's not even get *into* the planets. That's when it all becomes terrifying for a decade or two, not just that there are other planets, which is awful enough upon first hearing, but that there are also other suns. That just seems so wrong. What a nightmare—not just a few other suns, but *dozens* of them. No, this can't be, it's too much. Then it turns out that there are hundreds of other suns, and then thousands. You could have a nervous breakdown at seven years old trying to take this in, and then again at eight when you learn there are also a hundred other universes. This is so terrible, worse than finding out that your parents have sex (or at least did, those three times).

The only good news is that we somehow ended up on the one planet where someone thought up Monopoly and Oreos. By the time you discover that there are millions of other galaxies, you also discover boys, and then, even better, beer, Sylvia Plath, rock and roll. Things begin to look up. You may be able to give this joint a run for its money. This is when Wow means *Phew*.

There are movies you never forget, whose scenes and music imprint themselves onto your being. For me, it was *Elvira Madigan*, which I saw at thirteen with my best friend in a shared two-hour wow. People have said, laughing, things like, "Oh, it was basically like a shampoo commercial," and I say, "Aren't you great to try and correct my memories for me?" I still love Mozart's Piano Concerto No. 21. I'm sorry; sue me. I just do. The experience was so romantic and beautiful that it stunned and haunted me: God.

When Sam was six or so, he explained to me why we call God "God": "Because when you see something so great, you just go, 'God!'"

I said, "God!" over and over when I went to New York for the first time, and when I saw a bay in Mexico carpeted with dolphins. I said "God" at my own house when a family friend, a man of eighty, recited Eliot's "The Love Song of J. Alfred Prufrock" one drunken evening with twenty old friends gathered around. That tableau is like a thumbprint on my heart.

People tell you stories over the years of such astonishing mystery or perfidy that you never forget them. Ten or fifteen years ago, my friend Neshama, who had just gotten back from Mexico, told me about one full-moon night while she was there: In the town square was a bull ring, with people drinking beer and being boisterous and incredibly loud, and bulls shuffling around in the dust, and music blaring, and food pouring out from everywhere. Four blocks away, in the front yard of a house, a family was trying to pull a big black tarp upright to create some privacy. But even with the tarp you could see that in the yard were a hundred wreaths and pots of flowers, hundreds of candles ablaze, and a wooden casket with someone's body in it. People were milling around the yard and the coffin, chairs were being set up, and the people were going to sit up with the deceased all night, being in the presence of the person and the body and the memories.

I can perfectly remember the details and Neshama's face as she told the story, aghast at the bullfighting, aglow in describing the crummy yard bright with candles and flowers, mostly marigolds, whose yellow petals symbolize the sun, and light the path by which the departed soul finds its way back to the living.

When all is said and done, spring is the main reason for Wow. Spring is crazy, being all hope and beauty and glory. She is the resurrection. Spring is Gerard Manley Hopkins, "The world is charged with the grandeur of God. / It will flame out, like shining from shook foil." I read Hopkins for the first time in seventh grade, when I also first read Langston Hughes, and between the two of them, I was never the same.

Poetry is the official palace language of Wow.

Buds opening and releasing, mud and cutting winds, bright green grass and blue skies, nests full of baby birds. All of these are deserving of Wow—even though I have said elsewhere that spring is also about deer ticks—and everywhere you look, couples are falling in love, and the air is saturated with the scent of giddiness and doom. Petals are wafting and falling slowly through the air, and there is something so Ravel, languorous, reminding me to revel in the beauty of things wafting.

And autumn ain't so shabby for Wow, either. The colors are broccoli and flame and fox fur. The tang is apples, death, and wood smoke. The rot smells faintly of grapes, of fermentation, of one element being changed alchemically into another, and the air is moist and you sleep under two down comforters in a cold room. The trails are not dusty anymore, and you get to wear your favorite sweaters.

In spring, we expand and stretch in all directions. It's green exuberance and giddiness, bright clown colors and Easter colors, too; the rebirth of the tender growing soul. In fall we hunker down, pull the purse strings of ourselves tighter, because it's getting darker and the storms are coming.

Nature explodes in winter and even more people die than in other seasons. The poor freeze and starve. It absolutely blows your mind how cruel nature and poverty can be. You almost have to turn away, and many people do. We see the brutality of life and nature, and also of what lives inside us. I don't like to see this. It does not work for me.

We try to do our best, and then a whole snowy hillside buries a thousand people. Life is eruptions, spasms, just as in our families. If you keep your heart open, these traumas beat you down. But against all odds, something emerges from the wreckage in our hearts, so we can bear witness: collect donations for the families, or the town where the fire broke out; to childhoods destroyed by charming tyrants; to miners trapped two thousand feet down.

Love falls to earth, rises from the ground, pools around the afflicted. Love pulls people back to their feet. Bodies and souls are fed. Bones and lives heal. New blades of grass grow from charred soil. The sun rises.

What can we say beyond Wow, in the presence of glorious art, in music so magnificent that it can't have originated solely on this side of things? Wonder takes our breath away, and makes room for new breath. That's why they call it breathtaking. We're individuals in time and space who are often gravely lost, and then miraculously, in art, found.

In art, we feel the breath of the invisible, of the eternal—which Elie Wiesel described in *Night* as "that time when question and answer would become ONE." Wow, what horror that man saw, and what beauty, truth, and silence he still managed to create from it. In paintings, music, poetry, architecture, we feel the elusive energy that moves through us and the air and the ground all the time, that usually disperses and turns chaotic in our busy-ness and distractedness and moodiness. Artists channel it, corral it, make it visible to the rest of us. The best works of art are like semaphores of our experience, signaling what we didn't know was true but do now.

In museums, when we behold framed greatness, genius embracing passion, obsession, discipline, and possibly madness, our mouths drop open. For a short time, we see past all that is jumbled, mysterious, marvelous, and ugly. Instead, we glimpse life, beauty, grief, or evil, love captured and truth held up to the light. Art makes it hard to ignore truth, that Life explodes and blooms, consumes, rots and radiates and slithers; that eternity really is in a blade of grass. Jethro Tull sang that the same God who made kittens also made snakes in the grass. We stand before Monet and Rothko and the Sphinx and Georgia O'Keeffe and are speechless, in awe. Awe is why we are here. And this state is the prayer: "Wow."

To watch one dance number by Fred Astaire or Pina Bausch is to see the sacred in communal energy. We see where everything comes from and where it all passes through—childbirth and death; the glorious, graceful, immediate, brutal; all that bad behavior. We see where everything is headed: more childbirth, more death, more bad behavior. We see in art a moment in time, an instant, and this is holy.

"Wow" has a reverberation—wowowowowow— and this pulse can soften us, like the electrical massage an acupuncturist directs to your spine or cramped muscle, which feels like a staple gun, but good. The movement of grace from hard to soft, distracted to awake, mean to gentle again, is mysterious but essential. As a tiny little control freak, I want to understand the power of Wow, so I can organize and control it, and up its rate and frequency. But I can't. I can only feel it, and acknowledge that it is here once again. Wow.

Even though I often remember my pastor saying that God always makes a way out of no way, periodically something awful happens, and I think that this time God has met Her match—a child dies, or a young father is paralyzed. Nothing can possibly make things okay again. People and grace surround the critically injured person or the family. Time passes. It's beyond bad. It's actually a nightmare. But people don't bolt, and at some point the first shoot of grass breaks through the sidewalk.

The words "wow" and "awe" are the same height and width, all _w_'s and short vowels. They could dance together. Even when, maybe especially when, we don't cooperate, this energy—the breath, the glory, the goodness of God—is _given_.

Gorgeous, amazing things come into our lives when we are paying attention: mangoes, grandnieces, Bach, ponds. This happens more often when we have as little expectation as possible. If you say, "Well, that's pretty much what I thought I'd see," you are in trouble. At that point, you have to ask yourself why you are even here. And if I were you, I would pray "Help." (See earlier chapter.) Astonishing material and revelation appear in our lives all the time. Let it be. Unto us, so much is given. We just have to be open for business.

Sometimes—oh, just once in a blue moon— I resist being receptive to God's generosity, because I'm busy with a project and trying to manipulate Him or Her into helping me with it, or with getting my toys fixed or any major discomfort to pass. But God is not a banker or a bean counter. God gives us even more, which is so subversive. God just gives, to us, to you and me. I mean, look at us! Yikes.

God keeps giving, forgiving, and inviting us back. My friend Tom says this is a scandal, and that God has no common sense. God doesn't

ANNE LAMOTT

say: "I have *had* it this time. You have taken this course four times and you flunked again. What a joke." We get to keep starting over. Lives change, sometimes quickly, but usually slowly.

Another thing to hate: I would much prefer quick dramatic change, as long as it was for the better. But unfortunately, a lot of us don't experience Pentecost—tongues of fire appearing over our heads, blasting us into a new dimension. That would be great if I had a little heads-up and if the timing was more convenient.

If we stay where we are, where we're stuck, where we're comfortable and safe, we die there. We become like mushrooms, living in the dark, with poop up to our chins. If you want to know only what you already know, you're dying. You're saying: Leave me alone; I don't mind this little rathole. It's warm and dry. Really, it's fine.

When nothing new can get in, that's death. When oxygen can't find a way in, you die. But new is scary, and new can be disappointing, and confusing—we had this all figured out, and now we don't.

86

New is life.

If you are like me, you'd like to be able to understand and describe life better. Then you could manage and control it and maybe realize a small profit or advantage. But that would be death. And when you see that you have mostly stopped trying to do this, and are instead trying to remember to step outside when you're buggy and to look up, you say "Wow." You mindlessly go into a 7-Eleven to buy a large Hershey's bar with almonds, to shovel in, to go into a trance, to mood-alter, but you remember the first prayer, Help, because you so don't want the shame or the bloat. And out of nowhere in the store, a memory floats into your head of how much, as a child, you loved blackberries, from the bram- bles at the McKegneys'. So you do the wild- est, craziest thing: you change your mind, walk across the street to the health food store, and buy a basket of blackberries, because the answer to your prayer is to remember that you're not hungry for food. You're hungry for peace of mind, for a memory. You're not hungry for cocoa butter. You're hungry for safety, for a moment

when the net of life holds and there is an occasional sense of the world's benevolent order.

So you eat one berry slowly, savoring the
sweetness and slight resistance, and after sucking the purple juice off your fingers you say:
Wow. That tasted like a very hot summer afternoon when I was about seven and walked bare-
foot down the dirt road to pick them off the
wild blackberry bushes out by the goats, Pedro
and Easter, in the McKegneys' field. Wow. The
blackberries tasted like sweet purple nectar, not
dusty exactly, but dusted just right, not quite
leafy but still alive, a little bitter around the seed,
juicy and warm with sunshine.

AMEN

A men" is how most of us end our prayers, the standard response to prayers in the synagogue and the church and the mosque. The word means "And so it is" or "Truly."

Well, that's very nice, but what on earth does "it" mean? *What* is? The people praying are the ones saying "Amen," so it's not God saying bossily, like Judge Judy, "So it is. All done. Go away. Get some help with that anger." It is us, the damaged, hopeless people, lifting up our hope, hate, gratitude, fear, and shame, saying, Boy, do we hope we are right about this God stuff.

Someone has a baby, or pulls the trigger, or snatches the money, or picks up the drink or doesn't, or makes it to the shore, and everything sorts itself out, or falls apart, and through it we pray, Help, help, help. Thank you. Wow. Amen. . . . And then two hours or two days later, Help. We are saved by memories of love and beauty—maybe there's more of that to come, if we keep on keeping on. Or we are haunted by our failures and mortality, and beg that we not end up in such darkness again, so we say, "Amen." Life is motion, change, stagnation, bloom; nothing ever seems to happen, or awful stuff happens, or beautiful stuff happens, and we say, "Amen." Just when we think we've gotten things all lined up nicely, a rogue wave washes it all away, or deposits onto the shore a bright orange queen conch that we've been looking for all our lives, or a big chunk of fossilized whale bone, honeycombed with minuscule cells of color, and we say, "Wow." We're blown away, for a time, and then we usually slip back into regular old life.

And so it is.

The Amen is only as good as the attitude. If you are trying to finish up quickly so you can

check your cell phone messages, you are miss-
ing the chance to spend quiet moments with
the giver of life and the eternal, which means
you may reap continued feelings of life racing
along without you. So as Samuel Beckett ad-
monished us to fail again, and fail better, we try
to pray again, and pray better, for slightly longer and with slightly more honesty, breathing
more, deeper, and with more attention.

Quiet, deep breath after any prayer is another form of Amen.

We pray without knowing much about
whom we are praying to. We pray not really
knowing what to pray for. We pray not
really knowing how to pray. Certain Christians,
who will happily tell you they have a monopoly
on truth, say that Jesus gave us exact instructions of how and what to pray: the Lord's Prayer.
Isn't that nice? Thank you, Christians. Love
that certainty. It must be great to be so sure of
yourselves all the time.

Matisse actually said the most useful thing
I've ever heard about praying: "I don't know
whether I believe in God or not. I think, really,

I'm some sort of Buddhist. But the essential thing is to put oneself in a frame of mind which is close to that of prayer."

So maybe we bow our heads and close our eyes, and let our chins drop to our chests. Or maybe we lift our hands, palms up. Or perhaps we crumple to our knees, at the very end of our rope, and we cry out, like crazed people, "God help me." Or we sit quietly in a sacred room, elbows touching our neighbors', and we listen prayerfully and say, "Lord, hear our prayers."

Shelley, my friend of fifty years, and I hike and run to the top of a great foothill many mornings, and when we first see the peak of Mount Tamalpais, we shout, "Hello, Mother," sort of like the March daughters in *Little Women*, and Shelley does a Native American shimmying cheerleader bow and scrape. That's a prayer.

I love to pray at the beach, staring out at the surf and the pelicans, my prayer at those moments "Oh my God, oh my God." I try not to bog down on the "my" or "God" part of this prayer. It is the "Oh" that matters, the expulsion of air from the lungs, that occasional gorgeous shock

at what tiny molecules of the whole we are, com-
pared with, say, ten feet of shoreline at Stinson
Beach, which may be one of the most beautiful
places in the universe.

The tide comes in and sweeps out our children's castles, and it hurts so much, and a wave
knocks our father over, and he injures his back;
he'll never be the same. We pray to be of so-
lace, and to find the courage to let people have
their feelings. We breathe and pray to stay silent
while people find their own way through. (Well,
we try.) We pray to stay calm when the earth
shakes and explodes. The universe is always
having spasms and eruptions. It's labor. That's
how things get born. We rush in to help.

I pray not to be such a whiny, self-obsessed
baby, and give thanks that I am not quite as bad
as I used to be (talk about miracles). Then something comes up, and I overreact and blame and
sulk, and it feels like I haven't made any progress at all. But it turns out I'm less of a brat than
before, and I hit the reset button much sooner,
shake it off and get my sense of humor back.
That we and those we love have lightened up

over the years is one of the most astonishing sights we will ever witness. Your father, playful and *listening?* It's like Lourdes around here.

I pray for the change in perception that will let me see bigger and sweeter realities. My friend Mason, who is fifteen and has brain cancer, had a massive bleed eighteen months ago. He was in a coma and then for many months in a deeply silent condition where it seemed to me, but not to his mother, that he was brain-damaged.

One day his mother e-mailed me a video from Mason's rehab hospital in Texas, titled "Mason Singing." My heart leapt. His brother had filmed him in music therapy, sitting in a wheelchair between his mother and his thera-pist, who was playing "He's Got the Whole World in His Hands." At the end of every line, Mason would make a sound that was close to "hands," and everyone cheered. I inwardly groaned, hav-ing imagined something so different, so much better.

Later that morning I went up alone to my praying place. I called out, "Hello, Mother." Then I prayed for a glimpse of wisdom.

By the time I got to the bottom of the hill, I was amazed that Mason, silent for so long, had sung.

There is singing, and there is singing. Mason is back in school now.

We religious types, even those who detest organized religion, pray for deeper faith and a greater sense of oneness with God. Once when I was about to fly to the other side of the world and asked my church for prayers, my pastor said, "By the time you get on a plane, it's too late for beggy prayers. It's time for trust and surrender." These two things are almost all I want, but unfortunately, neither one is my strong suit. I am very strong on blame, and wish this were one of God's values, but trust, surrender? Letting go, forgiveness? Maybe just after a period of prayer, but then when the mood passes and real life rears its ugly head again? Not so much. I hate this, the fact that life is usually Chutes and Ladders, with no guaranteed gains.

I cannot will myself into having these qualities, so I have to pray for them more often, if I want to be happy. I have to create the habit, just as I had to do with daily writing, and flossing.

I read a lot about people of faith, how they sought union with God, and blessed however it came. There was for instance a man of God named Pedro Arrupe, who was elected head of the Jesuits in 1965. He was Basque, and he spent many years as a missionary in Japan. He was there when the atomic bomb was dropped on Hiroshima. Arrupe was deeply influenced by Japan, emotionally and culturally and spiritually. In his later years, he had a series of strokes. Soon after they began, he wrote in his journal, "More than ever I find myself in the hands of God. This is what I have wanted all my life, from my youth. But now there is a difference. The initiative is entirely with God. It is indeed a profound spiritual experience to know and feel myself to be totally in God's hands."

To have prayed to know God's care firsthand, without mediation, and to give thanks for the gift. To know that God's maternal hands hold one's life, like a baby. That is so not me, and is really all that I want.

I think often of Raymond Carver's poem "Late Fragment," written before his death at fifty, inscribed on his tombstone, almost too well-known to bring up again, but I have to:

> And did you get what
> you wanted from this life, even so?
> I did.
> And what did you want?
> To call myself beloved, to feel myself
> beloved on the earth.

Amazing things appear in our lives, almost out of nowhere—landscapes, seascapes, forgiveness—and they keep happening; so many vistas and so much healing to give thanks for. Even when we don't cooperate, blessings return to our lives, even in the aftermath of tragedy.

Things get a little better when we ask for help. People help us. Most astonishing of all, people forgive us, and we eventually forgive them. Talk about miracles. The kids turn out to be okay after all. The widow finally gets back on her feet. If you're like me, you ask your higher power for help, and then cause further *need* for help by procrastinating, or refusing to cooperate with simple instructions that follow sincere petition. And yet even so, grace, progress, blessings continue to be given to you, because God gives. It's God's job.

How can that *be*?

C. S. Lewis wrote: "I pray because I can't help myself. I pray because I'm helpless. I pray because the need flows out of me all the time, waking and sleeping. It doesn't change God. It changes me." I have heard this passage in a number of sermons in far-flung churches over the years. "It changes *me*." Hearing this makes me less afraid and more grateful, less critical and more trusting.

More than anything, prayer helps me get my sense of humor back. It brings me back to my heart, from the treacherous swamp of my mind. It brings me back to the now, to the holy moment, whether that means watching candles float on the Ganges or bending down in my front yard to study a lavish dandelion, delicate as a Spirograph drawing, that looks like its very own galaxy. Amen amen amen!

So I pray constantly between bouts of trying to live life on life's terms. Help. Thanks. Wow. I end most prayers with Amen, before my inevitable reentry into regular old so-called real life, because for thousands of years believers and prophets have *said* to.

So I do. It's that simple.

You've heard it said that when all else fails, follow instructions. So we breathe, try to slow down and pay attention, try to love and help God's other children, and—hardest of all, at least to me—learn to love our depressing, hilarious, mostly decent selves. We get thirsty people water, read to the very young and old, and listen to the sad. We pick up litter and try to leave the world a slightly better place for our stay here.

Those are the basic instructions, to which I can add only: Amen.

Let it happen! Yes! I could not agree more. Huzzah. It is a good response to making contact with God through prayer, and to praying with people who share the journey, and to most things that are good, which much of life can be. So it is, when we do the best we can, and we leave the results in God's good hands. Amen.

Acknowledgments

Thank you, my friend Liping Wang at the Wylie Agency. Thank you, Geoff Kloske, and thank you, everyone at Riverhead, for everything. Anna Jardine, thank you: you are the best copy editor ever, and I'm sorry I told everyone you have unresolved precision issues, because without you, everyone could see that I am a college dropout.

Thank you, Neshama Franklin, Doug Foster, and Tom Weston, for frequent, invaluable help. You are my collaborators. Thank you, Mark Childress, Karen Carlson, Janine Reid, Steven Barclay, and Kathryn Barcos.

Thank you, St. Andrew Presbyterian Church, in Marin City, California, and Rev. Veronica Goines and the Amen corner: I am here because of you, and love you more than I can ever say. Thank you, Sam Lamott and Jax Lamott: you are the two best reasons I can think of for having a life.